Series title: BLACK LEADERS IN THE FREEDOM
STRUGGLE

PAUL

ROBESON

by Marie Stuart

Illustrated by Deborah Weymont

This book is part of a series written by Marie Stuart (Tyrwhitt) and published in her memory.

Marie wanted stories about the lives of these brave people to be more widely known. She believed that such stories would serve to encourage those facing the same challenges today.

Published in 1993 by Marie Tyrwhitt Publications©, by Bristol Community Education Service, Stoke Lodge Centre, Shirehampton Road, Stoke Bishop, Bristol BS9 1BN with the sponsorship of relatives, friends and colleagues of Marie Tyrwhitt.

Reprinted in 1998.
Reprinted in 2002

Printed by Printing & Stationery Services, UWE, Bristol.

Marie Stuart, the author of the books in the Black Leaders in the Freedom Struggle series, was a teacher of adults and children and a writer throughout all her long life. She was also a learner and one who believed that to be really alive means to be growing and changing. To do so means that we must be free. Free to question and free to find our own answers and our own way.

Marie Stuart wrote these books out of a passion for freedom for all, regardless of race, colour or creed, and out of a deep admiration for the heroes celebrated in this series. They are 'heroes' not because they conquered great empires, but because, by their actions and their example, they gave something of great value to the liberation of their people. They stood up and took their place proudly amongst the human race, having struggled heroically against the disadvantages to which they were born. These stories and those lives will never die as long as we have the courage to strive for our human right to dignity and equality and the generosity to realise that the breath of freedom is sharing. It is in that spirit that these books should be read and in loyalty to the memory of those brave black leaders in our freedom struggle.

PAUL ROBESON

1898-1976

Chapter One

Paul's Roots

Paul Robeson was a great singer of Black songs, or spirituals. Here are his own words about what singing meant to him:

If I can create for an audience the great sadness of the Negro slave in *Sometimes I Feel Like a Motherless Child,* or if I make them know the strong, gallant convict of the chain gang, make them feel his thirst in *Water Boy,* his simple divine faith in *Weepin' Mary,* then I shall increase their knowledge and understanding of my people. They will sense that we are moved by the same emotions, have the same beliefs, the same longings, that we are all human together..... If I can teach my audience to know about the Negro through my songs, then I will feel that I am using my art for myself, my race, for the world."

This is just what he did, and because of this his people must not forget him or his songs.

Paul's father William was born a slave in North Carolina, U.S.A. The surname Robeson came from Robertson which was his master's name, for at that time most slaves had no surname of their own. However, William made up his mind that he was not going to be 'Robertson's William' all his life. He was a lad of spirit, and at the age of fifteen, he risked the dangers of running away. Helped by the Underground Railway[1], he made his way North and managed to find a job. Although he was very intelligent, he had only been to the plantation school as a little boy. Now he wanted to get a real education, so he went to night school after each day's work. His ambition was to become a preacher. So he saved hard, and with the help of a scholarship, was able to work his way through to Lincoln, a college for black people. Here he passed his exams, and in time became a pastor in a Presbyterian Church in Princeton, New Jersey. He married a teacher, the daughter of another Presbyterian minister. They had five children; the

---

[1] The 'Underground Railway' was another word for a network of people whose homes or 'stations' were used as safe places to pro-vide temporary shelter for escaping slaves.

youngest, Paul, was born on April 9th, 1898. At that time his father was fifty-three years old.

Although Princeton was less than fifty miles from New York, the people who lived there were just like those who lived in the Deep South (or Dixieland). This was because after the Emancipation when the slaves were set free, many of them came to the North to find work. As most of them had very little education, the only work they could find was as servants in the houses of the rich whites. So they were cooks, waiters, caretakers, coachmen, labourers on the nearby farms and in the local brick-works.

Many of Paul's relations, his uncles and aunts and cousins, were workers like this because his father had found jobs for them amongst his rich parishioners. He was the pastor of the church which had been built by white people. As the Reverend William Robeson he was respected by them. He was a fine preacher and they enjoyed his sermons. So he was loved and respected by black and white alike; he acted as their go-between and could move freely amongst them all. He helped black people to find jobs. He gave advice to those who needed a lawyer. He gave out the cast-off clothes of the rich to those who could not afford to buy any.

However, although the white community respected him, his children had to go to the segregated school. His eldest son had to travel eleven miles a day to go to a High School for black students because only white people could attend the one in Princeton. And when this same son wanted to go to Princeton University he was denied a place because he was black. Yet at the same time, the President of the University had just been granted the Nobel Peace Prize!

After Paul was born, his mother was in poor health. Then his father lost his job as pastor through no fault of his own. With an invalid wife and five children to support, most men would have gone under. Not so the Reverend William Robeson! As if to prove that a man could still keep his dignity while working in a lowly job, he got himself a horse and wagon and earned his living as an 'ashman' (as garbage collectors were called in those days, because they collected ashes from the house fires before there were gas or electric fires or central heating). He also acted as coachman for the black students of Lincoln College. In spite of his humble job he was still respected and loved by the black community. He did not complain, and worked hard to see that his children had a good education. The eldest boy was to be a preacher, the next a doctor, and the only girl a teacher.

Then fate struck again. Paul's mother was the victim of a terrible accident in which she was burned so badly that she died. Paul was only six at the time. However, he got plenty of mothering, not only from 'Pop' and his brothers and sister but from all his relations. "Across the road and down the block were aunts, uncles and cousins" he wrote in his autobiography. He was adopted by them all. "There was always a place at the table and in a bed, often with two or three others" when his father was away on one of his coachman trips to the sea-shore or attending a church conference. They were all hard working and mostly poor. Their food was simple - greens, black-eyed peas and cornmeal bread. But "they had a hearty appetite for life." From them he learned the songs, hymns and ballads of the Negro spirituals.

"I heard my people singing," he wrote, "in the glow of the parlour coal-stove and on summer porches sweet with lilac air, from choir loft and Sunday morning pews - and my soul was filled with their harmonies."

Paul's father was always there for him too. They spent most evenings together. Father would ask his young son about his school work. He always expected him to do well, not because he wanted him to be top of the class but because he wanted him to get the best out of himself. They had fun together, too. Pop liked to play a game of checkers and they would sit for hours over the game, not speaking much but very happy together. His father never spoke to him about his own childhood as a slave, and Paul found it hard to believe that such a noble man as his father had ever been *owned* by another man as if he were a horse that could be bought and sold. Years later, a man came up to Paul after one of his concerts, thanking him for making the name of Robeson famous. "Your father used to work for my grandfather," he said. Paul replied, "You say my father used to work for your grandfather. Let's put it this way. Your grandfather exploited my father as a slave." And that was the end of the conversation.

Chapter Two

The Start of a Stage Career

When Paul was nine years old, his father, then sixty-two, was able to go back to preaching. He was made pastor of an African Methodist Church in another town, so they moved away from Princeton. Here Paul went first to a Black elementary school, and then to a high school which gave places to a few black students. He was very intelligent and hard-working, and most of the white teachers were helpful and friendly to him. He soon became popular with the white students too, because he was very good at all sport - football, baseball and boxing.

In his final year at the high school Paul heard of a competition which was open to all students in New Jersey. The prize was a four-year scholarship at one of the best and oldest colleges in America. Paul entered for it because he wanted to prove that he was as intelligent as a white student. And he won! He looked upon it as a victory for his people. At first he had to put up with some jealousy shown him by the white students, but he won them over by his friendly nature. Also, his excellence at all forms of sport was a help.

While he was still at the university his father died. Paul missed him a lot, for he had loved his father dearly. However, he stayed on to finish his course and graduated in 1919. He was then chosen as one of the four men of his year who were "outstanding in scholarship, athletics and personality in this famous white university." It was a very great honour not only for Paul but for his people. On that occasion he made a speech on 'International Relations.'

What was to be his next step? With his father gone there was now no family home, as a new preacher was in the parsonage. So where was he to go? What was to be his career? He thought of the law and decided to study at Columbia University. But first he had to earn the money to pay for his fees and keep. So he went to Harlem, the Black quarter of New York, and worked as a waiter, in the Post Office, as a coach for basketball teams, and he played professional football (He could earn as much as a thousand dollars a game). He was even tempted to become a professional boxer.

Then, at a party, he met a gifted young black woman named Eslanda Goode. She had just graduated from a teachers' college. They fell in love and got married in 1921. Essie, as she was called, taught while Paul went on with his studies. He graduated from law school in 1923 and found a job in a law office. However, he soon gave this up because the other, white, lawyers objected to his being there. So he drifted along, doing casual jobs as before.

Then he was asked to take part in a play which was being acted at the Y.M.C.A. in Harlem. It was called *Simon the Cyrenian,* and he played the part of the black man who carried Christ's cross. It so happened that a famous playwright named Eugene O'Neill asked Paul to take the leading part in a play he had just written called *All God's Chillun' Got Wings.*

The story was about a black man who married a white woman, an unheard-of thing in those days. Several New York papers condemned the play as being un-American. The Klu Klux Klan tried to prevent it from being acted, and Paul was in danger of being lynched. However, in the end the play was given a run, and, although it was not a success, Paul's acting in it was highly praised by the theatre critics. They hailed him as a "born actor." In the next few years he acted on the stage and made such films as *Emperor Jones, Show Boat* and *Sanders of the River.* However, Paul knew that the parts he would be able to play as a black actor were very few. So he felt that he could not really make a career of acting. What then?

Again luck came his way through a chance meeting in Greenwich Village, the arts area of New York. This time it was another black man, named Lawrence Brown, who sparked things off. Brown had just come back from Europe where he had become famous as a compiler of songs called *spirituals.* He and Paul at once became friends.

Of course Paul knew these songs from his childhood days. His eldest brother Ben tells in a letter how the family found out that their young brother had something special about his voice. He wrote, "The family had just finished dinner, the day was hot and sultry. We began to lounge comfortably in our common den, when suddenly Bill suggested that we strike up a few tunes. We started out with gusto, Bill, Paul and I. We went through our repertoire - everything from *Turkey in the Straw* to *Silent Night.* We were making one of those minors known only to home-loving groups. Paul was bearing down on it with boyish glee, in fact all of us were. Out of the discord, Bill yelled 'Wait a minute. Hit that note again Paul!' Paul hit it out of the lot and Bill said, 'Paul, you can sing.' 'Stop kidding me, boy,' replied Paul, laughing it off."

They broke up for a game of baseball in the lots, but when they returned home Bill asked Paul to sing the old song *Annie Laurie.* He listened carefully and at the end repeated, "Paul, you can sing."

Paul thought it was a joke, but from then on he began to sing in the choir of the church where his father was a

minister. He also sang at church concerts and at the Glee Club in high school, but he never had any formal singing lessons. However, Ben claimed that Paul's singing career really started that July afternoon with the three brothers singing round the table. "Without that happening," he wrote, "I doubt if he would have ever been near any singing group."

Chapter Three

Growing Awareness of Racial Injustice

Without that lucky meeting with Lawrence Brown, the world might never have heard that wonderful voice. Of course Brown soon discovered that Paul had this rare gift. Then the two of them went into partnership - Brown to play the piano accompaniment and Paul to sing. They arranged for a concert to be given in New York. The programme consisted of sixteen black songs, mostly spirituals. Paul had found his vocation.

He told himself that he would use his voice and the spirituals to help break down the barriers that had been imprisoning his race for centuries. He saw in these spirituals the very soul of his people that had been formed "through all the long weary years of their march towards freedom." He said, "That spirit lives on in our people's songs, in the sublime grandeur of *Deep River,* in the driving power of *Jacob's Ladder,* in the militancy of *Joshua Fit the Battle of Jericho* and in the poignant beauty of all our spirituals."

After the first concert the press was full of praise. One musical critic wrote that Paul's voice was "the finest musical instrument wrought by nature in our time." Another said that his voice was "the greatest basso voice of our present generation which can be felt as a physical force."

After this first success, Paul and Lawrence Brown toured the United States with their spiritual concerts. Up till that time Paul had not travelled much in his own country - he had been too busy getting his education. Now he became even more aware of the racism that existed in his own country and what segregation meant for the working man. Even he, privileged as he was because of his fame, could not eat in many first class restaurants or register at first class hotels. And sometime he could not get tickets on the first class Pullman trains, though his wife Essie, who was light-skinned, could buy them. He felt angry at being treated as a second class citizen.

In 1925 O'Neill's play *Emperor Jones* was brought to London, with Paul playing the lead. Essie came with him, and here, for the first time, the young couple were able to live where there was no official colour bar. It gave them a freedom of movement that they had never know before. The same was true when they paid a visit to France. On their return to New York they found the restrictions that were enforced there even more irksome.

Soon they were back in London again - indeed, Paul made so many friends there that he felt like making it their permanent home. He loved talking with the black students at London University, and learned from them about the colonialism that was going on in Africa. He met and talked with some of the African leaders such as Kwame Nkrumah and Jomo Kenyatta. He learned about African history and its culture, and even began to learn some of the African languages. As he listened he came to feel that it was not only the ex-slaves in America who were demanding full freedom but that all over the world colonial people were fighting for the same right.

Of course, wherever he went he gave concerts with Lawrence Brown and always drew huge audiences. It was as a singer that most people knew and loved him. But then he was asked to play the part of Othello in Shakespeare's play. It was to be put on in London and all the other players were to be famous English actors. Since Paul had not been trained as an actor, he at first refused. However, in the end he agreed, because, he said, "The play is modern, for the problem is the problem of my own people. It is a tragedy of racial conflict, a tragedy of honour rather than jealousy. Othello's colour heightens the tragedy."

Paul's acting brought the tragedy across as no other man's acting had ever done. In the past the part of

Othello had always been played by a white actor with his skin blackened. To have a black actor play the part made it far more real. Paul's performance was a huge success. There were twenty curtain calls after the first show! Yet when he returned to America, the play could not be produced because of stirring up racism.

So it was not surprising that during the next fifteen years he spent much of his time touring Europe, giving concerts and stage performances. He often came to London and other cities in England. But he also went to most of the other European countries, France, Germany, Italy, Spain - and Russia. He enjoyed being there and even began to learn to speak Russian because, he said, he "never had to worry about his personal freedom there and never had a single slight because he was a black man." He never became a communist, but he did arrange for his little son, Pauli, to spend two years at school in Moscow. All the later years of Pauli's education took place in America, but these two years in Moscow were held against Paul later on during the anti-communist years of McCarthyism.

One country he did not visit again after Hitler came to power was Germany. He was very anti-Nazi. He said, "In what way was the burning cross and white robes of the Klu Klux Klan different from the Swastika and Brown-shirts of Hitler?" But he did go to Spain in 1938 during the Civil War there and sang for the International Brigade. He saw the struggle for Black civil rights as part of the anti-Fascist struggle.

When the second world war started in Europe in 1939, Paul, Essie and Pauli went back to New York, as America did not take part in the war till several years later. This meant that Paul was cut off from his friends in Europe except by letter and phone.

Chapter Four

An Unsilenced Voice

Shortly after the war started, the USSR became an ally in the fight against Nazi Germany and suffered terrible losses (twenty million dead). But as soon as the war was over there was a great fear of the spread of Communism in America. People who were thought to be communists were brought before the House of Representatives Committee on Un-American Activities. Paul was one of these because he was known to have often visited Russia and to be friendly towards that country. It was remembered that he had sent his only child to be educated there.

In his defence Paul said, "I stand here struggling for the rights of my people to be full citizens of this country. They are not - in Mississippi. They are not - in Montgomery. That is why I am here today. You want to shut up every coloured person who wants to fight for the rights of his people." And he repeated, "I speak as an American Negro whose life is dedicated first and foremost to the winning of full freedom and nothing less than full freedom for my people in America."

Paul's way of fighting was through his singing and acting. He was an artist, not a soldier or a politician. He felt that through his art he could make white people know what it meant to be treated as a second class citizen. However, although he swore under oath that he was not a communist, the Committee declared that he was a dangerous man who could stir up trouble by rousing world feeling against America's 'Jim Crow Laws.'[2] So they took away his passport.

This meant that he could no longer go abroad to give concerts. It robbed him of the most important years of his life as an artist and made it more difficult for him to earn his living. He had done what he could during the war years to help the fight against the Nazis by giving concerts in America for the sale of War Bonds. Now the fear of Communism made many of his white American friends turn against him.

However, Paul went on singing, writing, and making speeches for what he felt to be his mission. As one newspaper put it, "Robeson's cry is for justice, happiness

---

[2] Jim Crow Laws were laws which segregated black and white people in every aspect of life and death.

21

and freedom here and now, while we live, not in some far away time in the future. His is the voice that shouts down promises of bye and bye and bellows Now! Now!"

Here is one of the old songs from slavery days that he sang:

"My old master promised me
When he died he'd set me free.
He lived so long that his head got bald
And he gave up the notion of dying at all."

The audience joined in the singing, and then Paul asked, "How long must we wait?" His answer was, "As long as we permit it . . . we ourselves have the power to end the terror and to win for ourselves peace and security throughout the land."

Although Paul had earned a lot of money by his singing and acting, he now felt he had much more in common with the working class than with the rich white people. After all, he had come from a working class background and many of his relations were working class people. It made him angry that a black worker only got half as much pay as a white one for doing the same job. Thinking about how unfair this was made him interested in Trade Unions. So when he was invited to sing for a Convention of Trade Unions in Canada, he agreed to go without charge. Americans did not need a passport to go

to Canada, and he thought there was nothing to stop him. However, the State Department thought otherwise and told him he could not go over the border. So the Canadians arranged for the meeting to take place at Peace Bridge Park on the border between Canada and America. Thirty thousand Canadians came for miles around to hear him sing and to protest against his being barred from entering their country. The same thing happened for the next three years until the State Department finally gave way.

Another way in which Paul was able to defy the ban was by using the telephone. For instance, he was able to sing to an audience of Welsh miners at an Eisteddfod.

Perhaps the most important project he was able to take part in was by invitation of the World Federation of Trade Unions. He was sent the words of some songs they wanted him to sing. They were in German, so he translated them. They were about Peace and Freedom and the Brotherhood of the working people of all lands - just the things that Paul felt most deeply about. He was given only the notes of the tunes and told that the musical accompaniment would be added later. He had to time them to the exact second so that they would fit into the sound track of a film for which they would be used. The film was being made in Holland.

Well, it was quite an undertaking! At that time Paul lived in Harlem, New York. He had no studio and no technician to make the recording, but his son Pauli, now a young man, was a very good electrician, so he was able to do this.

Another problem was finding somewhere quiet enough. Paul's own place was much too noisy. In the end his brother Ben, now a minister, let him have his study in the parsonage. Then everyone in the family was told to be very quiet. "Ssh! Uncle Paul is trying to make a record." There were interruptions - a knock on the door, a plane overhead - but at last it was finished. The tape was packed in a box and sent off to an unknown address - that was, unknown to Paul.

It finally appeared in a Dutch film called *Song of the Rivers.* The accompaniment to Paul's singing was by a famous Russian composer, Shostakovitch, and the words of the songs were by a famous German poet and playwright named Berthold Brecht. The commentary was by a noted French novelist, and the poster to advertise it by the great artist Pablo Picasso. Six countries - Holland, Germany, Russia, France, Spain and America - had together made a work of art for Peace. It was translated into many languages and shown all over the world. Paul must have felt very happy to be included in this in spite of the ban on his being able to go abroad.

At last, as a result of a petition that was started by the Actors' Equity Association, Paul's passport was returned to him. He was then almost sixty years old. He began giving concerts abroad again, and at first the music critics said his singing was even better than as a young man.

Sadly, in spite of his splendid body as a young man, the years had taken their toll. His health began to fail. He was visiting Russia in 1959 when he became seriously ill and had to be taken to hospital in Moscow. When he got better he went to London, but fell ill again and was in and out of hospital for the next four years. In between, he tried to give concerts and even to act Othello again, but the old Paul was gone. His voice was shaky - shaky! Paul's voice! He was a pale shadow of the man he had been. His career was over.

In 1963 Paul and Essie came home to the United States. He was a tired, old man. He died in 1976, but his voice can still be heard on tapes and records, and these are his best epitaph. For "in his singing he championed the cause of the common man." As his college President once said of him when making a speech about Paul's contribution to humanity, "You sing as if God Almighty sent you into the world to advocate the cause of the common man in song."

And as Paul himself said, "I came here to sing, and for you to sing with me."

Series title:
BLACK LEADERS IN THE FREEDOM STRUGGLE

Titles published

Sojourner Truth

Frederick Douglass

Josiah Henson

Harriet Tubman

Booker Washington

Marcus Garvey

Toussaint L'Ouverture

The Wonderful Adventures of Mrs Seacole

Mary Seacole

Martin Luther King

and an introduction: Slavery in America